Poetry

Shrinking Days, Frosty Nights

Poems about Fall

by Laura Purdie Salas

Capstone press®

Mankato, Minnesota

2

Watchman

Stay out of our

Crops or I will get

Angry — crows, grackles, and sparrows too!

Robbing our harvest is

Ever so rude, thinking our

Corn and our wheat is for you. Fly away,

Race to some other farm, to filch your

Oats and seeds for free. Find yourself an empty field

Without a scary guard like me!

3

Score!

Grab a helmet, wear your cleats, call the play with rhythmic beats.

Ready!
Set!
Hike!

Time to start the playoff game. Run the ball to touchdown fame.

5

Big Yellow Ride

The first day of school
Is finally here
Fill up my backpack
To start off the year

Pose for a picture
While Mom and Dad fuss
Hurry outside to be
First on the bus!

Flying

The leaves have bid summer goodbye

They're resting here — brittle and dry

They crackle and crunch

When I gather a bunch

And toss them back up to the sky

Desk

I am   smooth wood

          pencils

I am   paper

          glue

I am   answers

          apples

I am   waiting

          for

you!

Apples

We don't just hang here, enjoying the view
We have lots of jobs, and here are a few:

Tree-sprucers
Sweet-juicers
Ground-spillers
Pie-fillers

Which of these sounds like the most fun to you?
What do you think of the fall jobs we do?

12

No Square Meals

Shrinking days, frosty nights, winter's coming, hay is bound. Rye and clover, dried and round, brown and round. Sheep will munch on winter dinners from the harvest, rests in rolls on autumn ground.

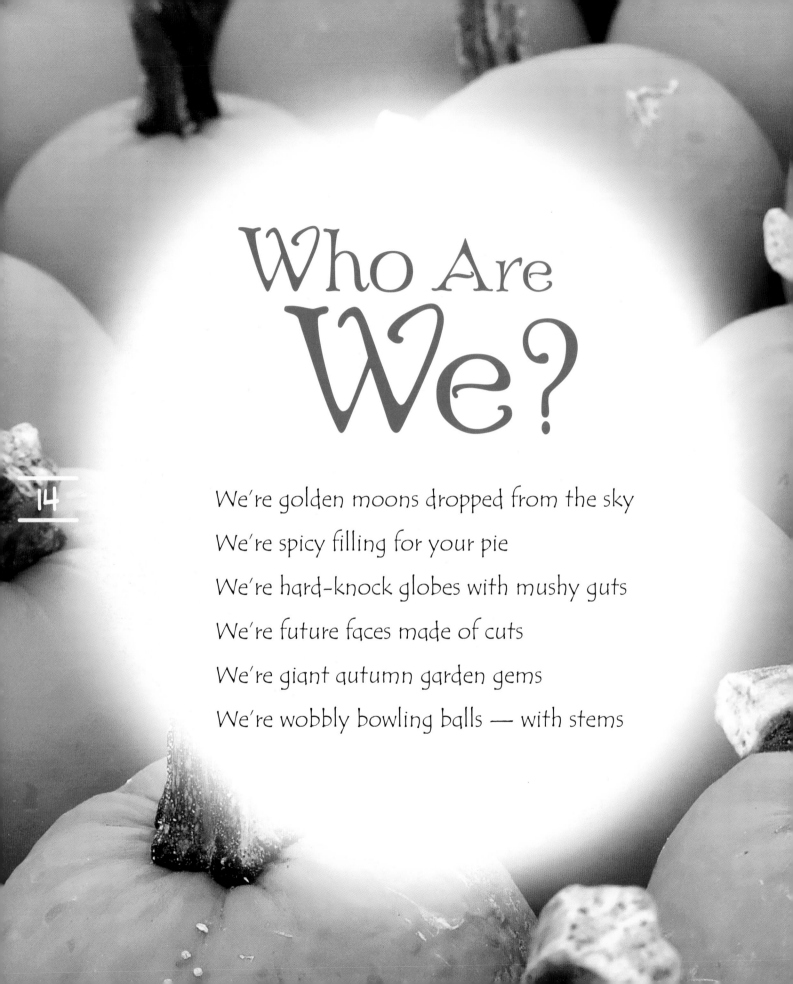

Who Are We?

14

We're golden moons dropped from the sky

We're spicy filling for your pie

We're hard-knock globes with mushy guts

We're future faces made of cuts

We're giant autumn garden gems

We're wobbly bowling balls — with stems

15

Still

Black cat

Becomes autumn —

Cold, slinky, inky night

Gold, glowing eyes like harvest moons

Watching

Midnight

See my spooky, blank eyes staring?

Like the crooked teeth I'm baring?

Feel my wicked candle flaring?

Am I smiling? Am I glaring?

Test the face that I am wearing:

Am I strange enough for scaring

you?

BOO!

18

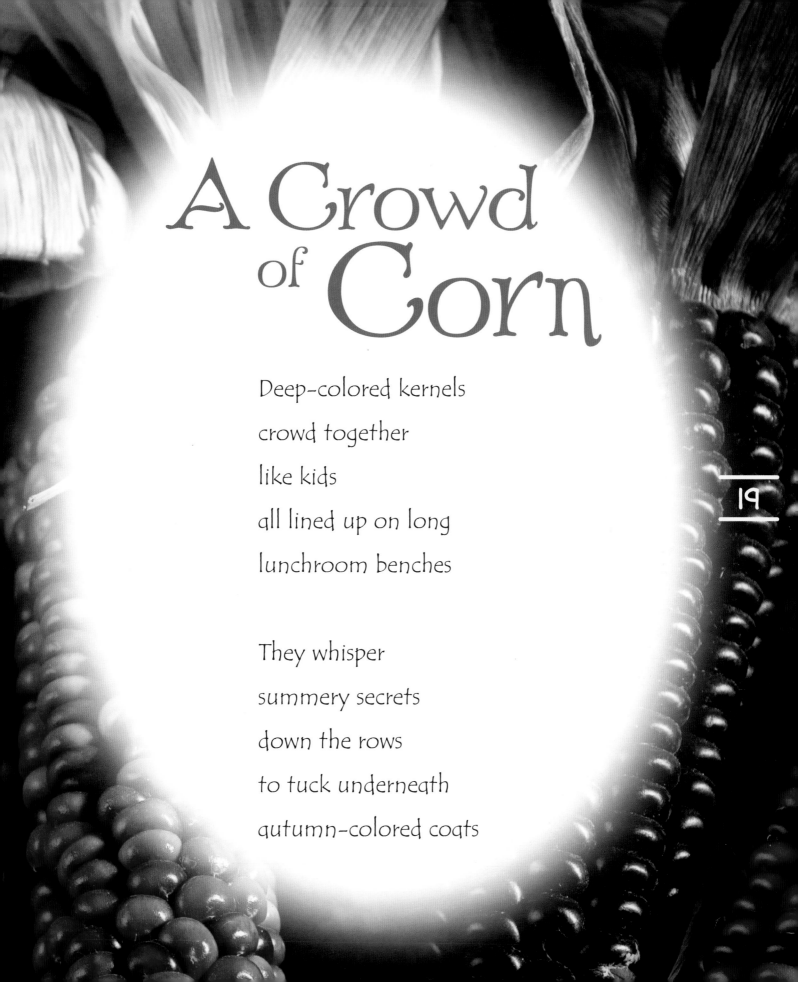

A Crowd of Corn

Deep-colored kernels

crowd together

like kids

all lined up on long

lunchroom benches

They whisper

summery secrets

down the rows

to tuck underneath

autumn-colored coats

Morning

Overnight, autumn

decorates delicate leaves

with glitter frosting

Preparing

Nights are stretching long and dark

Days dissolve much quicker

Autumn chill comes chasing now

Squirrel's fur grows thicker

Buried under crispy leaves

Squirrel finds a treasure

Tucks it in his hiding place for

Winter dining pleasure

21

Finally

I'm thankful

for my puppy

and his soft and watching eyes

I'm thankful

for my sister

even though she always cries

I'm thankful

for my baseball

and the sneakers on my feet

I'm thankful

dinner's ready

so I finally get to eat!

24

Up Here

Autumn is "it"

Chasing us through the sky

Pressing against our feathers

With each flap of our wings

We push the chill away and

Fly south

We are almost safe, home

We have escaped the cold,

Left it behind to chase someone else

Day's End

orange lights flickering,
orange windows bright,
orange skies decorate
autumn-glow night

orange jack-o'-lanterns,
orange falling leaves,
orange nights steal away
summer like thieves

The Language of Poetry

Couplet — two lines that end with words that rhyme

Repetition — the use of a word or phrase more than one time

Rhyme — to have an end sound that is the same as the end sound of another word

Rhythm — the pattern of beats in a poem

Acrostic

The subject of the poem is written straight down the page. Each line of the poem starts with one letter of the word. "Watchman" (page 3) is an acrostic poem.

Cinquain

A poem with five lines. The first line has two syllables. The second line has four, the third has six, the fourth has eight, and the last line has two syllables. "Still" (page 16) is an example of a cinquain.

Concrete Poem

A poem in which the words are shaped like the subject of the poem. "Score!" (page 4) is a concrete poem.

Free Verse

A poem that does not follow a set pattern or rhythm. It often does not rhyme. "Up Here" (page 25) is an example of free verse.

Haiku

A short poem that describes a scene in nature. It has five syllables in the first line, seven syllables in the second line, and five syllables in the third line. "Morning" (page 20) is a haiku.

Glossary

bare (BAIR) — to show

bound (BOUND) — tied up with rope or string

brittle (BRIT-uhl) — easy to snap or break

cleat (KLEET) — a shoe with small tips on the bottom to help football players stop or turn quickly

delicate (DEL-uh-kuht) — easy to break

dissolve (di-ZOLV) — to disappear into something else; day dissolves into night.

filch (FILCH) — to steal

globe (GLOHB) — anything round or shaped like a ball

grackle (GRAK-uhl) — a bird with shiny black feathers

harvest (HAR-vist) — to gather crops that are ripe; harvest can also be the crops that are gathered.

kernel (KUR-nuhl) — a single grain or seed of corn

pose (POHZ) — to stay still so that you can be photographed

shrink (SHRINGK) — to become smaller

slinky (SLIN-kee) — smooth and flowing

spruce (SPROOSS) — to make something look nicer

Read More

Esbensen, Barbara Juster. *Swing around the Sun*. Minneapolis: Carolrhoda Books, 2003.

Frank, John. *A Chill in the Air: Nature Poems for Fall and Winter*. New York: Simon & Schuster Books for Young Readers, 2003.

Internet Sites

Facthound offers a safe, fun way to find Internet sites related to this book. All of the sites on FactHound have been researched by our staff.

Here's how:

1. Visit *www.facthound.com*

2. Choose your grade level.

3. Type in this book ID **1429612053** for age-appropriate sites. You may also browse subjects by clicking on letters, or by clicking on pictures and words.

4. Click on the **Fetch It** button.

FactHound will fetch the best sites for you!

Index of Poems

Apples, 10

Big Yellow Ride, 6

Crowd of Corn, A, 19

Day's End, 26

Desk, 8

Finally, 22

Flying, 7

Midnight, 17

Morning, 20

No Square Meals, 13

Preparing, 21

Score!, 4

Still, 16

Up Here, 25

Watchman, 3

Who Are We?, 14

A+ Books are published by Capstone Press,
151 Good Counsel Drive, P.O. Box 669, Mankato, Minnesota 56002.
www.capstonepress.com

1 2 3 4 5 6 13 12 11 10 09 08

Library of Congress Cataloging-in-Publication Data
Salas, Laura Purdie.
   Shrinking days, frosty nights: poems about fall / by Laura Purdie Salas.
   p. cm. — (A+ books. Poetry)
   Includes bibliographical references and index.
   Summary: "A collection of original, fall-themed poetry for children accompanied by striking photos. The book demonstrates a variety of common poetic forms and defines poetic devices" — Provided by publisher.
   ISBN-13: 978-1-4296-1205-0 (hardcover)
   ISBN-10: 1-4296-1205-3 (hardcover)
   1. Autumn — Juvenile poetry. 2. Seasons — Juvenile poetry. 3. Children's poetry, American. I. Title. II. Series.
PS3619.A4256S57 2008
811'.6 — dc22   2007022403

Credits
Jenny Marks, editor; Ted Williams, designer; Scott Thoms, photo researcher

Photo Credits
Capstone Press/Karon Dubke, 2–3, 9, 10–11, 14–15, 18–19
Corbis/Bryan F. Peterson, 26–27; Stuart Westmorland, 20
Getty Images Inc./Panoramic Images, 24; Sean Justice, 23; Yellow Dog
   Productions, 6
Shutterstock/coko, cover, 1, 28; Dwight Smith, 12; Fribus Ekaterina, 17;
   Gary Paul Lewis, 5; Jaimie Duplass, 7; kevin bampton, 21; Lucy Wright, 16

Note to Parents, Teachers, and Librarians
Shrinking Days, Frosty Nights: Poems about Fall uses colorful photographs and a nonfiction format to introduce children to poetry and celebrate the season of fall. This book is designed to be read independently by an early reader or to be read aloud to a pre-reader. The images help early readers and listeners understand the poems and concepts discussed. The book encourages further learning by including the following sections: The Language of Poetry, Glossary, Read More, Internet Sites, and Index of Poems. Early readers may need assistance using these features.